Daughter

Daughter

poems by

Maureen Eppstein

Finishing Line Press
Georgetown, Kentucky

ACKNOWLEDGMENTS

Versions of some of these poems, sometimes with different titles, first
appeared in the following journals:

Bellowing Ark: "The Quickening"
Convolvulus: "Fallen Sticks," "Remnants"
Moving Out: "Presences," "Requiem," "Rite of Passage"
Willawaw Journal: "Daughters"
Writers of the Mendocino Coast Anthology 2021: "Hearts and Flowers"

or in these previous collections:

Earthward: "Fledging Day"
Horizon Line: "Empty Nest," "Not a Good Mother," "Wedding Day"
Rogue Wave at Glass Beach: "Leaving New Zealand"

About the Cover
The ten-inch high clay sculpture pictured on the cover is by
Andrea Gardner from her series "Small Stories."
Her website is https://www.andreagardner.co.nz/

Publisher: Leah Huete de Maines
Editor: Christen Kincaid
Cover Art: Maureen Eppstein
Author Photo: Nona Smith
Cover Design: Elizabeth Maines McCleavy

Order online: www.finishinglinepress.com
also available on amazon.com

Author inquiries and mail orders:
Finishing Line Press
PO Box 1626
Georgetown, Kentucky 40324
USA

Contents

I. A Stone in the Belly

Hearts and Flowers

My aunt demands we view her daughter's
glory box stacked high with nuptial linen.
In pride of place a tablecloth embroidered
with border of hearts and roses linked.
I bend to compliment the tidy handiwork
and catch a smirk of sibling rivalry
directed at my mother. Cousin
plans to wed the boy next door.

I too was offered marriage in that summer.
Mother would be furious if she knew
I turned him down. He was a lovely man
and would become in later years
a pillar of the town. But I
was scarce eighteen and college-bound.
I saw myself across a table from my cousin
sipping tea from dainty saucered cups,
the hearts and roses on her cloth
a chain-link fence imprisoning our lives.

Having It All

Nothing stings sharp as indulgent laughter
when you're twelve and harbor big ambitions
so you hide them deep and slowly learn to master
ways that other girls accept tradition:
absorb those fifties pop songs on the radio
that offer love and marriage as the plan
for normal girls, encourage you to know
your female role as helpmate to a man.

At twenty-one you think you have it all:
degree, a writing job, engagement ring,
plan to accumulate the wherewithal
to go abroad and jointly spread your wings.
  Problems and setbacks you anticipate
  But blithely disregard the role of fate.

New Bride, 1960

Ignorant of anything to do with sex
mother too shy to speak of it
too far away

friends steered me to a clinic
what a neat vagina they cooed
here's a nice little cap

I cried in the john
when it wouldn't go in
and the rats scratched at the wall

then every night the struggle
and the spermicide
each morning washing out the slimy gunk

whether that night the diaphragm failed
or whether I forgot to put it in
I do not know

pregnant
new husband furious
I'd sabotaged his plans

passage overseas already booked
my dreams of literary fame
also in shreds

I ventured old wives' remedies
hot baths (though lacking gin to drink)
long walks

found myself on sleazy streets
remembering when first I heard the word
abortion

girl I knew in high school
moved to city
seduced by married man

septicemia
cops phone her parents
Come get your kid. She's dead.

wondered
how one found
abortionists

frightened of my thoughts
I scurried home and learned to love
my parasite

The Quickening

The touch is delicate
like a petal
brushed
against the wrist
but not
accidental
a message
that initiates you
to a mystery
and you know
beyond book-learning
beyond
the sonogram's
blurred proof
that the message comes
from another being
inside yourself
 but not
your self
a new life
asserting itself
like a green shoot
shattering
its hard, black seed

Don't Make a Fuss

What is it like when my water breaks?
The doctor laughs at my ignorance.
Just don't call him at three a.m.
I'll have plenty of time, he says.

The doctor laughs at my ignorance.
I wake to blood on my gown, on the sheets.
I'll have plenty of time, he says.
Cold rain lashes the window.

I wake to blood on my gown, on the sheets.
Should I call the doctor my husband asks.
Cold rain lashes the window.
Nearest phone is a call box down the street.

Should I call the doctor my husband asks.
Don't make a fuss is my ingrained rule.
Nearest phone is a call box down the street.
The time is two forty-five.

Don't make a fuss is my ingrained rule.
Another towel between my legs.
The time is two forty-five.
I say there's no need to call.

Another towel between my legs.
More towels ooze red in the tub.
I say there's no need to call.
By morning the baby lies low and quiet.

More towels ooze red in the tub.
Something's wrong screams the voice in my head.
By morning the baby lies low and quiet.
I tell myself she's not dead, but sleeping.

Something's wrong screams the voice in my head.
No baby's cry in the birthing room.
I tell myself she's not dead, but sleeping.
Through a blur of anesthesia the doctor's voice.

No baby's cry in the birthing room.
A gray pall shadows the bed.
Through a blur of anesthesia the doctor's voice:
Get that thing out of here.

A gray pall shadows the bed.
He'd said don't call him at three a.m.
Now only grief like a stone in my belly
Tells what it's like when my water breaks.

Monster Mother

As in the tale of the Ancient Mariner, the maternity home aide clutched my arm as she shuffled me past the birthing room door on our way to the bathroom. Eyes glittering, voice a conspiratorial whisper: *I'm not supposed to tell you this. I was there.* Her body quivered, as if the memory was fetid and slimy with rot. *You wouldn't have wanted to see that baby. The head was huge, all pushed out of shape. The rest of it limp as a rag doll.* Her claw tightened on my arm. *A terrible thing. Just as well it died.*

Weeks later, the autopsy report. Nothing wrong with the baby. No hydrocephalus. Enlarged head merely the result of forceps and the pulling out of tissue already dead. Which left me a monster for not seeking help, my guilt like a slaughtered albatross heavy about my neck.

Injunction

Do not mourn
the child that lived
only in awareness of maternity

Do not flinch
at the hammer-blow
shock of discovering death and life
stalking in kinship

Do not question
the empty womb
or the unfulfilled
loneliness of the breast

Do not condemn
the giving
and taking away

Nothing More to Say

My baby died

silence   my punishment

my own silence   others'
    silent discomfort

    frail condolences   crumple
like flowers

before the steel door

        of my face

       uncle shushed

   for noting my pallor

She's been ill, dear
from aunt who lost two at birth

nothing more
      to say to me

the baby died
         nothing more
     to say

Leaving New Zealand

I am Katherine Mansfield come again
on that slow ship out of Wellington.
Taste of bile in my mouth, I endure
airless heat of lower decks rank
with galley smells and deep-throated
thump of engines.
The ice-slick of my daughter's death
stumbling my speech,
I sit with parties playing Scrabble on the deck
where Indonesian stewards in white jackets
rattle tea-trolleys.

Evenings, I watch for that streak of light
as sun plunges into viscous sea.
Then sudden dark.
Familiar stars of my Antipodes
recede southward.
In their place, carved mahogany panels
fill walls of staterooms and stairways:
solemn eyes of strange beasts
peer from behind carved vines,
birds in extravagant plumage
perch on the edge of my dreams.

Tug of War

I want a baby, says woman's belly.
I want to be Famous Writer, says head.
But I want a baby, says belly.

Shut up and let me write, says head.
Your writing sucks, says belly.
You're right, says head. You win.

Cremation

Winter afternoon
onto hot coals one by one
manuscript pages

II. Healing Ground

Rite of Passage

There was no rite of passage when my daughter died
stillborn   unnamed
a cemetery bill
a hideous memory
a quarter century of guilt and anger
carried deep   like a rough-edged stone

until that day
work colleagues gathered in a conference room
to learn the words to greet
one of our number whose newborn also died
I spoke
the stone shifted
a question
suddenly it rose
tore through my gut   my throat   my mouth

they held me, sobbing, as it rolled away

Presences

Ancient presences are here already
on this healing ground
merged with new foliage of the oaks
soft grass   lupine flowers

one by one we draw more women
into the circle of shared heritage
mothers   grandmothers   daughters

"I am Maureen
  daughter of Gweneth
    grand-daughter of Lilian ..."

suddenly there you are

        "mother of Jane who died at birth"

named at last
and leading by the hand
all our other lost children
whose mothers' hidden griefs
we share in sisterhood

Requiem

I walk again the path
I walked last year
after you came to me
daughter who died at birth
my long drought of grief is over
soft rain sweeps
like a benediction over the hills

at the place beside the stream
where ancient healers left
memory of their mysteries
I touch cool water to my face
you are here
  in the water
        in the grass
  in the flowers
        in the trees

stay in peace

Fallen Sticks

Sticks white as infants' bones litter deep duff
here in this corner hard by the main gate
of Bromley Cemetery,
but hidden from view by massive cypresses.
I've brought no flowers.
There is no slab for them to wither on.
Beyond this corner, tight-packed
ranks of gravestones halt abruptly,
marking a boundary
between the public dying and the deaths
not spoken of.

It took me thirty years to come.
I stand imagining
the undertaker with a tiny box,
a hasty spade,
remembering how hastily I also
hid the knowledge that connects me to this place.
I drink in details,
knowing I may never come again:
trash caught in the hedge,
broken branches sinking back to earth,
low sunlight catching shallow dimples
where some bird or rodent has been digging.
Also blackbirds singing,
sparrows coming home to roost.

Voices whisper:
We are many, babies in unmarked graves.
We lay quiet in each others' arms,
comforting each other. We became
the cypress cones and needles that have grown,
fallen and grown again.
We are the bird that eyes you from that patch of sunlight.
We are the rustlings in the hedge.

Leave your token anywhere, they tell me.
We are everywhere.
Under the largest tree I clear a patch of earth
and spell my daughter's name in fallen sticks.

Fledging Day

The moment opens like a gift:
infant swallows on wobbly wings
fledge from the porch-corner nest.

Their twittering glitters in ecstasy
of blue freedom, swoop and skim
of graduation caps flung high.

Hawk and raven lurk,
a long migration looms,
the art of catching insects in the air

yet to be mastered.
But for now, a whirl of swallow shapes,
a celebration.

Empty Nest

This morning I watched the swallows fledge,
the Violet-greens who each year nest
where cross-beam and roof timbers
meet in a corner of the porch.

Two round white bodies perched at the nest-cave edge,
two dark-capped heads peered out.
Of a sudden one took off
and then the other,

leaving me oddly bereft,
a feeling not quite grief—more sweet than that—
more a memory of that pensive pride
when human young depart the family home.

Such a short time the swallows have:
a few summer weeks to perform their frenzied
parental crescendo of nesting and feeding,
of swooping in and zooming out.
Then suddenly the task is done.

Such a short time we humans have
to feel the procreative energy that links us
to an interwoven chain of being,
to know the preciousness of feathered lives,
sunlight on an iridescent wing.

Wedding Day

Like steam that lifts
from damp earth after rain,
winged beings emerge
from a hole by the rotting stump.
Briefly the sunlit sky is full of them.

They find a mate then drop,
shrug off their wings
and march in tandem head to tail
to found another termite colony
underground.

The discarded wings
are exquisitely delicate,
a lacework of silver-gray
veining that shimmers
like finely-spun silk.

Grown to wear only once,
but that once an ecstasy
of urgent light
and filmy fluttering,
the wings are a wedding gown.

I am

I am birds that flutter round the feeder
      for I too am bones and flesh and beating heart

I am trees they perch in
      for I too am nourished by neighbors

I am stream where they drink
and sea to which it flows
      for I too am water

I am valley and mountain
      for their minerals are in me

I am the world
      and stardust from whence it came

Not a Good Mother

Our elderly cat likes
 to lie cradled like a baby
in my husband's arms

my husband was away
cat prowled the house
and yowled

if I were a good mother
I would have offered comfort
I was busy

so I muttered *Shut up, cat*
and knew kinship with those
whose babies fail to thrive.

Daughters

My stillborn daughter
disappeared for thirty years.

When finally I named her,
learned to mourn,
women the age she would have been
began to show up in my life
bearing other faces
other names.

Some of them would joke
and call me "Mom."
I'd laugh with them, imagining
I heard that unheard voice.

I loved them all
like daughters.

Remnants

May these arms that now cradle
remnants of ragged
guilt that hiss
like a gas burner the moment before light
lift upward, swing
into a sky made open.

Miraculous that words spoken can open
memory of an empty cradle
useless to swing,
bring out my ragged
sobs into the light,
my guilt receding like the shore waves' hiss.

Telling at last my his-
tory, I felt my body open,
releasing grief that like a stone rolled into light,
while a friend cradled
me in his arms and let my ragged
breath ease into a steady swing.

Only death is final. Memories swing
back to the hiss
of ignorant complicity and the ragged
contractions as my body opened
for a child that would never fill a cradle,
never see the light.

I cannot make light
of the pendulum swing
that lets me now cradle
for words like gold as sluice waters hiss
over grief once raw as rocks laid open,
the edges of memory ragged.

I want to render my ragged
tatters of grief into a substance light
as the leaves that lie open
to the sun and swing
with a sibilant hiss
in their airy cradle.

My cradled flame of memory is ragged,
but will persist until the hissing wick dims its light,
the sky swings open.

Maureen Eppstein's most recent poetry collection is *Horizon Line* (Main Street Rag 2020). Previous collections include *Earthward* (Finishing Line Press 2014), *Rogue Wave at Glass Beach* (March Street Press 2009) and *Quickening* (March Street Press 2007). *Quickening* was also first runner-up in the 2007 Finishing Line Press/ New Women's Voices competition. Her poetry has appeared in numerous literary journals and anthologies, including *Fire and Rain: Ecopoetry of California* (2018), and has been nominated for a Pushcart Prize. Crossing the boundary between the arts and the sciences, her poems have been included in a textbook on computer graphics and geometric modeling and used in a university-level geology course.

A fifth-generation New Zealander, she left her birth country as a young woman. After several years working as a freelance journalist in England, she immigrated with her husband and two young sons to the U.S., where they joined a community of high-tech transplants in what became known as Silicon Valley. She began writing and publishing poetry in the 1980s, fitting it in with a career as an administrative writer and editor at Stanford University and a volunteer role helping to run a monthly poetry reading series. On retiring to the northern coast of California, she became executive director of the Mendocino Coast Writers Conference and taught poetry workshops at College of the Redwoods. Her other interests include gardening and observing the wildlife around her home between the forest and the sea.

www.ingramcontent.com/pod-product-compliance
Lightning Source LLC
Chambersburg PA
CBHW022051080426
42734CB00009B/1300